HOW TO DUNK
IF YOU'RE UNDER
6 FEET TALL

*13 Proven Ways to Jump Higher
and Drastically Increase Your
Vertical Jump in 4 Weeks*

By James Wilson

TABLE OF CONTENTS

Introduction   1

Chapter 1 – What Is a Vertical Jump?   3

Chapter 2 – What Muscles Are Involved   9
in the Vertical Jump?

Chapter 3 – What Helps or Hurts the   13
Vertical Jump?

Chapter 4 – The Mechanics of the Dunk   17

Chapter 5 – Vertical Jump Workout   21
Program

    The 4 Week Training Program   37

Conclusion   43

About the Author   45

INTRODUCTION

Instead of spending your weekends going to the movies, hanging out with your friends, or maybe going on a road trip or two, you hang out at the gym or are glued to your computer, tablet, phone, or television watching every clip of video you can on dunks. Heck, your home is a shrine to the performances of Dr. J, Dominique Wilkins, Shaq, Michael Jordan, and Clyde Drexler. *The dunk is your obsession, your passion, and it's an integral piece of all things important in your world*.

Alas, there is a problem and it's a mighty big, or, shall we say, small, one? It's your stature. *At under six feet tall, there is no hope* you will ever know the true exhilaration *of slamming one down* through the net. You fantasize about it. You wake from vivid dreams at night in a cold sweat imagining your head above that rim, but you truly despair it will never happen. You will never be able to check that one all-important item off your bucket list.

Keep your chin up; there is hope for you yet! Sure, there are tons of programs hawked on the internet to improve your vertical leap so that even someone as short as 5'5" will be able to dunk the ball with ease, but you have a healthy dose of skepticism when you hear their claims. That can't really be true!!! I'm vertically challenged, and that is that; but, what if it was true? **What if there was a way to increase your vertical leap to the necessary level that you could dunk?** Wouldn't that be one of the most fantastic, powerful feelings you have ever experienced in your life? Of course it would; so pick up this book and start turning the pages, because all the information you need to achieve this esteemed goal lies within these paragraphs. Don't waste one more precious minute. Start reading!!!

CHAPTER 1 – WHAT IS
A VERTICAL JUMP?

On May 23, 2013, *DJ Stephens*, who hailed from the University of Memphis, was officially charted as possessing a ***46-inch vertical leap*** while trying out for the Brooklyn Nets. It was the highest leap ever recorded by the NBA draft combine, but still didn't necessarily put the 22-year-old on the path to a career in the pros.

The previous vertical jump champ, at least in the NBA, was thirteen years ago and his name happened to be *Kenny Gregory*. The former University of Kansas guard never played a minute in the NBA and spent his entire career either in D-League or abroad. Just to put it in perspective, **Michael Jordan and LeBron James both can jump about 44 inches**. At age 50, Michael still possesses some hops.

Looking at *Gregory* as an example and also referring to *Earl "The Goat" Manigault*, whom Michael Jordan, Earl Monroe, and Kareem Abdul Jabbar all said was "The Greatest Player to never make the NBA" and had a 52-inch vertical leap, this physical skill is not necessarily a requirement for a successful professional career rife with accolades, but as with anything in life, every little bit helps.

So let's take a look at exactly **what a vertical leap is, how it is measured, and if it indeed is something that can be improved**.

A **vertical jump**, or **leap**, is when a person lifts his or her center of gravity when moving vertically through the use of their own musculature. It simply is a quantification of how high an athlete can jump off the ground while standing still. There is also a running vertical jump.

The **easiest way to get a handle on how high someone's vertical jump is**, is to have that person stand with their feet flat on a level surface and have them reach with their hands as far up as they can on a nearby wall with their feet remaining on the ground. Mark this point. Then have the person jump several times and mark those heights on the wall. **When you measure the height between the two, that is the person's vertical jump**. Of course, there are more scientifically advanced ways to obtain this measurement by using sensors, lasers, and pressure pads, but more than likely, most of us will not simply have this lying around in the garage or in the locker room at the gym.

There are also applications on your smartphone you can use to measure your vertical jump. One example is the FitnessMeter by Stan Kaiser (itunes.apple.com/us/app/fitnessmeter-test-measure/id477488986). You do have to purchase it for $1.99, but you can also use it for other fitness-related activities. It uses your camera to measure the distance between the two points to calculate your jump.

Jump height from video or motion

There is also some more advanced equipment to measure your vertical jump.

According to most published information, here are the **average figures** for men and women when it comes **to** their **vertical leap**. It increases from about the age of 10 until just after high school and levels off the in the 20s for both genders. It is an excellent measure of lower body power.

rating	males (inches)	(cm)	females (inches)	(cm)
excellent	> 28	> 70	> 24	> 60
very good	24 - 28	61-70	20 - 24	51-60
above average	20 - 24	51-60	16 - 20	41-50
average	16 - 20	41-50	12 - 16	31-40
below average	12 - 16	31-40	8 - 12	21-30
poor	8 - 12	21-30	4 - 8	11-20
very poor	< 8	< 21	< 4	< 11

So after reviewing the basics of what a vertical leap is and how to measure it, the next step is *can you increase or improve it?*

If so, in what way?

Granted, your physique will always be based on genetics, so there will be a ceiling, and you may not be able to advance from a 19 to a 44, but you can improve your vertical leap. No, it doesn't involve an invasive surgery or a certified personal trainer. All you need to do is follow a specific exercise program and incorporate a diet that burns fat without decreasing muscle mass, and you will be well on your way to a new leap measurement.

CHAPTER 2 – WHAT MUSCLES ARE INVOLVED IN THE VERTICAL JUMP?

Okay. So you aren't six feet tall, and you still really, really want to dunk. In fact, you watch as much footage of dunk contests as you can and pore over all the information you can access. No worries, you don't have to be six feet tall to slam the ball home. Just look at *Spud Webb* and *Nate Robinson*. Webb at 5'7", which I think was a healthy listing, and Robinson at 5'9" are the only two players in NBA history to win the Slam Dunk contest and be under six feet tall.

So, how do you get started? Well, the vertical jump is characterized as an explosive movement, and there is a lot of literature available on that; but the muscles involved in the activity themselves have not really been examined as to how they interact during the exercise.

In *Mechanics of the Vertical Jump and Two-Joint Muscles: Implications for Training* published in 1998 by Dr. Brian Umberger MS, CSCS, of the Department of Orthopedics at the University of Rochester Medical Center, Umberger outlines **the movement is essentially one of two joints, the hip and the knee**, and exercises that can be used to improve it.

"Using the laws of classical mechanics," Umberger wrote. "It is possible to determine the net joint forces, net joint (torque), and joint powers generated during the vertical jump. **During the take-off phase, the net joint forces about the hip, knee and ankle are positive**, meaning the net effect of all the load-carrying structures (muscles, ligaments, joint capsules) will be to extend the hip, extend the knee, and plantar-flex the ankle. During this phase the joint powers are positive, indicating predominantly concentric activity of one-joint muscles."

"The take-off phase of the vertical jump begins with the extension of the hip joint, followed sequentially by the knee and ankle joints," he continued. "It ends when the feet lose contact with the floor. The take-off phase is preceded by the preparatory phase which involves flexion at the hip and knee joints and dorsiflexion at the ankle joint. Muscle activity is generally eccentric during the preparatory phase with gravity providing the driving force."

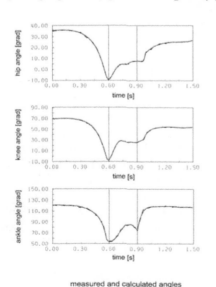

measured and calculated angles

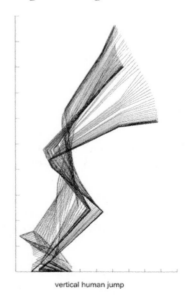

vertical human jump

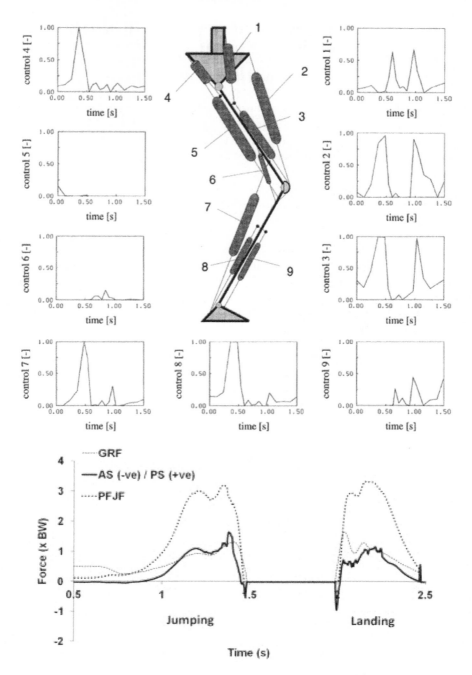

"If the vertical jump involves a highly orchestrated sequence of events that involve all parts of the lower extremity, then **exercises that stress the body**

in that fashion, such as the power clean and snatch, hang and clean, or plyometrics should be chosen," Umberger wrote. "In the clean and snatch care should be taken to emphasize the second pull as this is the portion that most closely represents the jumping motion."

"Although isometric movements are generally not a major portion of the strength program of competitive athletes, exercises that stress low or zero-contraction velocity may be indicated for athletes that perform many max intensity jumps, as these muscles must transmit very high loads at a low con-centration velocity during such jumps," he continued. "**Activities could also include, slow, heavy squats, or isometric squats in a safety cage. Other appropriate exercises could include slow, heavy heel raises, with the knees near full extension.**"

So Umberger's work provides us with a basic guideline. Not included in his work, however, is that your **core strength contributes to how strong your lower legs are** so that will be another area you will need to work on in order to improve your vertical jump. Also, based on Umberger's research, the **calves are not an integral piece of the leap puzzle. The muscles over the joints of the hip and knee bear most of the burden.**

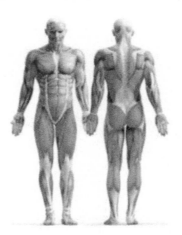

There are still several other questions about what can impact improving your vertical leap before we get into outlining a step-by-step instruction guide for exercises.

These inquiries include, do the shoes make a difference? Is there a diet to follow that might aid in our efforts? Is there a certain height I have to jump to get above the rim? Are there certain myths about what I need to do to improve my jump that I need to know the truth about?

CHAPTER 3 – WHAT HELPS OR HURTS THE VERTICAL JUMP?

On October 19, 2010, www.nba.com posted a notice banning its players from wearing a new line of **Footwear** by Athletic Propulsion Labs entitled the *Concept 1*. This shoe, with a $300 price tag, was fashioned around a spring-based mechanism that was created to escalate a player's lift while jumping.

"Under league rules, players may not wear any shoe during a game that creates an undue competitive advantage," the NBA officially stated.

Based in Los Angeles, the company was founded by former USC basketball walk-ons and twins Adam and Ryan Goldston, whose father just happened to be a former CEO at Reebok.

The shoes were also tested by *Sports Illustrated* columnist Chris Ballard. And guess what? **The shoes don't really help**. You have to work on your jump itself through physical exercise and form in order to jump higher.

Here are some myths about what kind of **exercise and diet** you can use **to increase your vertical jump**:

- *Creatine is bad for you* and illegal. **False**. This is produced naturally in the body and is used by many professional athletes to get the most out of their workouts. It increases the body's production of energy.

- *Protein shakes will stunt your growth*. Also **Untrue**. It just supplements what you receive from your diet and is essential to build muscle.

- *If you are experiencing muscle soreness from working out, you should push forward*. **No way**! Recovery is just as important in building your body as working out. Listen to what your body tells you. That is how you will achieve your fitness goals.

- *If you were injured in the past, you can't take part in a workout* to increase your vertical jump. **Partly true and partly false**. It depends on your injury, but with the advances of modern technology and medicine, it is highly possible you will be able to find a program that suits your needs without subjecting your body to further harm.

Let's delve into the **Diet** and discuss several things. First off, your **body fat does affect how high you can jump** and that makes perfect sense if you stop to think about it for a minute.

This is why it is necessary to maintain the perfect balance for proper fitness. The ideal amount of body fat is really relative to each person and what their needs are. If you feel you are not explosive enough, you might want to consider reducing your body fat. Average levels range from 5 to 20 percent.

There are also tools available online that can aid you in gauging and transforming your body fat levels. One of them can be found at: healthstatus.com/calculate/body-fat-percentage-calculator.

Also, here is a *chart* just *to keep body fat and its levels in perspective.*

Body Fat Percentage For Men

	Ideal body fat percentage for Men			
Age(yr)	Excellent	Good	Fair	Risky
20-24	10.8	14.9	19.0	23.3
25-29	12.8	16.5	20.3	24.3
30-34	14.5	18.0	21.5	25.2
35-39	16.1	19.3	22.6	26.1
40-44	17.5	20.5	23.6	26.9
45-49	18.6	21.5	24.5	27.6
50-54	19.5	22.3	25.2	28.3
55-59	20.0	22.9	25.9	28.9
60+	20.3	23.4	26.4	29.5

Body Fat Percentage For Women

	Ideal body fat percentage for Women			
Age(Yr)	Excellent	Good	Fair	Risky
20-24	18.9	22.0	25.0	29.6
25-29	18.9	22.1	25.4	29.8
30-34	19.7	22.7	26.4	30.5
35-39	21.0	24.0	27.7	31.5
40-44	22.6	25.6	29.3	32.8
45-49	24.3	27.3	30.9	34.1
50-54	25.8	28.9	32.3	35.5
55-59	27.0	30.2	33.5	36.7
60+	27.6	30.9	34.2	37.7

General Body Fat Percentages Categories (The American Council of Exercise)

Set realistic fat loss targets when establishing your personal weight loss program according to your body.

Category	Women (% fat)	Men (% fat)
Fitness	21-24%	14-17%
Essential Fat	10-12%	2-4%
Athletes	14-20%	6-13%
Acceptable	25-31%	18-25%
Obese	32% plus	25% plus

So how can you transition, enhance, or modify your diet to improve your vertical leap? It would be based around the premise that you need to burn fat and build your muscle. These two concepts are completely intertwined when it comes to lowering your body fat.

How to accomplish this:

- You do have to ***employ a caloric deficit***. Meaning cutting down on your calories and exercising to burn more. But it should only be slight so you don't lose muscle.

- You will need to ***ingest a high amount of protein*** to keep your muscle mass.

- Carbohydrates and fats need to be kept at a minimum.

- Be involved in some kind exercise program involving weights or resistance training.

- You need to ***get lots of sleep***. It helps your body maintain your immune system, and it reduces the possibility of wasting away your muscles.

- Eat lots of fruit, vegetables, fish, nuts, eggs, chicken, and lean meats. Also ***drink plenty of water***. Try to avoid any other drinks as much as possible.

- Eliminate sugars and starchy carbohydrates from your diet.

Remember you can increase your jump by incorporating a workout program that does involve weight training, but it is not necessary. It really depends on your body and what you feel comfortable with. Probably **the swiftest way to jump higher is to improve on your form**. This is something that is often overlooked, of paramount importance to increasing your vertical leap, and one of the first things a personal trainer will tell you.

CHAPTER 4 – THE
MECHANICS OF THE DUNK

*"**It** was in seventh grade,"* NBA All-Star Shawn Kemp told the *Lawrence Journal World* in 1998. *"They didn't allow us to dunk but I got one. The best dunkers are the little guys."*

Rather than explain **the mechanics involved in dunking a basketball**, it might be easier to just check out this video so you can equate the movements with something visibly tangible. It might make the technical part a whole heck of a lot easier!

Simply go to http://youtu.be/TzJEjd6l8ro

There are two ways to dunk:

Takeoff – One Leg

- Start by speed dribbling up to the basket. Take the legal 2 steps, holding the ball in your dunking hand.

- Propel yourself from your second step, jumping high and extending your arm, aiming for the rim to send the ball directly into the net.

- Land softly on your feet to ensure a safe landing.

Takeoff – Both Legs

- Start by speed dribbling up to the basket. Plant both feet in order to jump-stop approximately 1 foot from the rim.

- Hold the ball between your hands, extending your arms, aiming at the basket, then jump as high as possible.

- Keeping both hands on the ball, send it directly into the net.

- Land softly on your feet to ensure safe landing.

Practice Tips

1. Start with an adjustable height basket and set the hoop low, gradually increasing height over time.

2. Practice your dunks with a smaller ball first, a tennis ball then a volleyball, for example, then gradually progress to a basketball after you master your process.

3. Start your practice dunks using one hand. Once you feel comfortable, start practicing with both hands.

4. Study your favorite NBA players' form; note what they do. What is their approach? When do they begin to jump? Remembering these details will improve your dunk.

Just a few **quick tips to remember.**

Try to keep jumping up and touching the backboard and the rim to familiarize yourself with the feel. Also, many people find it easier to dunk coming off one leg and with one hand. Practice how it feels for you to hold the ball jumping towards the rim before you make your first attempt, and keep in mind, many of today's rims are breakaways, so it will come down towards the ground if you try to grab it.

CHAPTER 5 – VERTICAL JUMP WORKOUT PROGRAM

So now you're ready to get started and follow an entire program after reading about the diet, exercises, and results you will receive when you devote yourself to improving your vertical leap enough to finally dunk that basketball!

What's the first step? If you take a look at what is available on the internet, you will discover a plethora of programs that cost money and either guarantee or simply trumpet the results they will supply if you just break out your credit card. Choosing the right program or plan for you can be confusing. However, as in other areas of life, a specific goal can be met in multiple ways. The same is true for improving your vertical jump.

Despite how many different ways there are to jump higher, you will soon read about the **general principles helping numerous people improve their vertical jump and be better athletes**. Professional and Olympic athletes alike have employed these same principles. If you add them to your practice regimen, your vertical jump will definitely see improvement!

So all the tools you need are right here within these pages to achieve the results you seek and within the time frame you would like.

Sure, there are ways to increase your jump immediately, which rely on technique. Many NBA coaches have helped players instantly by modifying how they begin the jump and how they hold their hands when they approach the basket. Also, you need to keep your hips and knees up. This is about *how you use your core muscles*.

Remember, once you begin, to **incorporate the protein** and other necessary additions **into your diet** in order to **lower your body fat**.

The following exercises are what you will need to work on to get that vertical leap exactly where you want it to be!

Squats

Research has shown this is the single **most important exercise to increase your vertical leap**, and the lower you go, the more height you will gain. Form, not frequency, is key.

Place your feet firmly on the ground, evenly spaced apart with the toes pointed slightly out to hold the balance. Bring your body down to a seated position with arms held out in front and then back up.

Lunges

Second on the list is the lunge.

With your body straight, look straight ahead and keep your gaze locked on some object ahead of you. Place one leg out and step forward; lower your hips so that both your knees are at 90 degree angles. Always keep your knee above your ankle so as not to injure yourself. Return to your starting position and repeat with the other leg.

One Legged Squat

Similar to the standard squat, you would start this by standing with your feet comfortably apart directly below your shoulders with one foot slightly pointed out. Bring your body down to a squat with one leg kicked in front of you and both arms extended forward for balance. Bring yourself back up to standing and alternate to the other leg.

Deadlifts

Start with one barbell or two small barbells on the ground. Squat to pick them up with feet a comfortable distance apart and toes pointed slightly outward. Pick up the weights while bringing your body to a standing position with the barbell or barbells in front of you. Take your body to a squat with the proper posture, bringing the barbells down to the floor again. Repeat these steps and always make sure to be very careful and commit to proper form. Otherwise, you could seriously injure your back.

Plyometrics

A family of explosive exercises to improve your vertical leap, ***plyometrics is an exercise plan that includes such things as jumping exercises over and around cones***. Some of these are done with medicine balls and weights to teach agility while jumping. These are combined with the strengthening exercises. You can even **use boxes** or steps to jump up and down upon.

48-inch box jump

Stationary jump

27

Another sort of exercise you should add to your routine is **Isometrics**. This involves building the fast and slow twitch fibers in your muscles to *increase your explosiveness and/or speed.* These exercises are very popular not only in this realm but also in the fitness world.

Jumping Strength Exercises

— Deep Knee-Bends

Start in standing position. Slowly bend your knees and keep your back straight. Sink slowly into a squat position as low as is comfortable, then stand back up slowly. Start with 15 reps; increase by 5 (up to 20) and then by 10 (30, 40, etc.) reps over time.

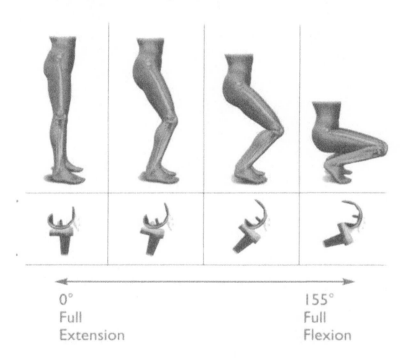

0°
Full
Extension

155°
Full
Flexion

— Knee-Bend Jumps

Follow the squat exercise described above, but for these jumps, you'll shift positions fairly quickly. You will almost touch the ground with your bottom, then explode up from the squat as high as possible. As soon as you land, repeat the squat and explode back up. Start with 15 reps; increase by 5 (up to 20) and then by 10 (30, 40, etc.) reps over time.

A.   **B.**   **C.**

— Toe Lifts

Start out standing on flat feet; lift your heels to stand on the very tips of your toes. Then, lower heels down to the ground. Do this slowly, not rocking up and down, but steadily. Perform between 30 and 50 reps.

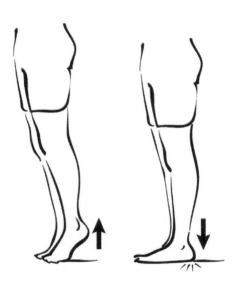

– Toe Lifts with Free Weights

Perform the toe lift exercise as described above while holding or wearing your free weights. Start out with smaller weights (for example, 5 or 10 pounds), gradually working your way up to heavier weights.

– Ab Crunches

It has been determined that sit-ups can injure your back, so try ab crunches instead. Ab crunches start with you lying on your back, and keeping it straight, then use your muscles to curl up by lifting only your shoulders off the ground. This slight modification is easier on your back and easier to repeat – perform continuous reps for 10 minutes twice a day.

— Jump Rope

Making this exercise a habit will definitely improve your vertical leap. Because the equipment is so mobile, you can literally jump rope anywhere, even while you watch movies, listen to podcasts, or catch up on your favorite TV series.

Static Stretching

This will be done after your workouts and on days off. It will help to maintain/increase your flexibility and assist you in recovering fully for your next workout. Get a timer and hold the stretches for the given amount of time without moving.

- **Hips stretch**: 1 minute per hip

- **Sitting hamstring**: stretch 1 minute

- **Sitting Quad stretch**: 2 minutes

- **Lying Gluteus stretch**: 1 minute per leg

— **Lower leg stretch**: 1 minute for each calf

— **Side splits attempt**: 30 seconds

- **Front splits attempt:** 30 seconds per leg

The 4 Week Training Program

You won't find a one-size-fits-all, miracle training program. You will need to apply the aforementioned general principles to increase your body's power-to-weight ratio and achieve flexibility that allow your body to get into the proper jumping positions, only then will your vertical jump improve. Despite the various programs and exercises that are available to help you achieve these goals, the "miracle" secret is to choose a program, stick with it, and see it through!

Keeping that in mind, **this program's goal** is to **enhance your flexibility, strength, and plyometric ability**. To do this, you will need to add weight to the aforementioned exercises every week and make the point to jump with as much strength and as high as possible for every rep.

Make sure you start with weights you can perform 4 x 12 reps easily.

WEEK 1:

Workout A

1. Dynamic Warm-up *(use a movement's speed and momentum to stretch the muscle(s))*

2. Squats – 4 x 12 reps

3. Lunges – 4 x 12 reps

4. Toe Lifts – 4 x 12 reps

5. Stationary Jumps (high as possible) – 4 x 7 reps

Workout B

1. Dynamic Warm-up

2. Deadlifts – 4 x 12 reps

3. One-Leg Squat – 4 x 12 reps

4. Deep Knee-Bends – 4 x 10 reps

5. Box Jumps (high as possible) – 4 x 7 reps

Take a 1-2-day break between these workouts depending on how you're feeling.

Do a static stretch and jump rope on days off.

WEEK 2:

Increase weight on each exercise by 10 lbs (about 5 kg) total

Workout A

1. Dynamic Warm-up

2. Squats – 4 x 10 reps

3. Lunges – 4 x 10 reps

4. Toe Lifts – 4 x 15 reps

5. Stationary Jumps (high as possible) – 4 x 8 reps

Workout B

1. Dynamic Warm-up

2. Deadlifts – 4 x 10 reps

3. One-Leg Squat – 4 x 10 reps

4. Deep Knee-Bends – 4 x 12 reps

5. Box Jumps (high as possible) – 4 x 8 reps

Take a 1-2-day break between these workouts depending on how you're feeling.

Do a static stretch and jump rope on days off.

WEEK 3:

Increase weight on each exercise by 10 lbs (about 5 kg) total

Workout A

1. Dynamic Warm-up

2. Squats – 4 x 9 reps

3. Lunges – 4 x 9 reps

4. Toe Lifts with Free Weights – 4 x 12 reps

5. Stationary Jumps (high as possible) – 4 x 10 reps

Workout B

1. Dynamic Warm-up

2. Deadlifts – 4 x 9 reps

3. One-Leg Squat – 4 x 9 reps

4. Knee-Bend Jumps – 4 x 10 reps

5. Box Jumps (high as possible) – 4 x 10 reps

Take 1-day break between these workouts.

Do a static stretch and jump rope on your day off.

WEEK 4:

Increase weight on each exercise by 10 lbs (about 5 kg) total

Workout A

1. Dynamic Warm-up

2. Squats – 4 x 8 reps

3. Lunges – 4 x 8 reps

4. Toe Lifts with Free Weights – 4 x 10 reps

5. Stationary Jumps (high as possible) – 4 x 12 reps

Workout B

1. Dynamic Warm-up

2. Deadlifts – 4 x 8 reps

3. One-Leg Squat – 4 x 8 reps

4. Knee-Bend Jumps – 4 x 12 reps

5. Box Jumps (high as possible) – 4 x 12 reps

Take a 1-day break between these workouts.

Do a static stretch and stomach crunches on your day off.

After you complete the program, take one week off; let yourself recover, then repeat the program. Make sure to start off with a weight you can perform 4 x 12 reps easily.

If you feel overworked or drained, take one day's rest and eat some healthy food. **Nutrition is as important as the training** when trying to improve the vertical jump.

If you do intend to push yourself hard and have some discipline, **I can guarantee that you will achieve the results you desire**.

CONCLUSION

After reviewing all the information, reading on your own outside of this book, and possibly speaking to others, you might finally be ready to pursue one of your dreams and increase your vertical leap enough to be able to dunk. It's certainly not impossible. In fact, it's a very attainable goal that can easily be reached in whatever timetable you choose so long as you are willing to put in the effort.

You should notice results after only one or two workouts, but after four or five workouts you will see a pretty significant improvement. You do not have to complete these exercises in any set order. I would recommend mixing them up throughout your various routines, not only to relieve boredom, but to constantly challenge your muscles. A good rule of thumb is to take at least one day off between each workout. If you stick to the program, you should be able to increase your vertical jump with a minimum three to six inches and a maximum of up to 15 inches.

Good luck, and when you implement these tips, exercises, and strategies, success truly will be yours.

You might never become his Royal Airness, but with this program, you can become the best athlete you possibly can be and start working on your signature jam!

ABOUT THE AUTHOR

James Wilson is a certified personal trainer and professional basketball coach. He has been developing young basketball players to excel in their game for over 30 years. He has worked with coaches and basketball players in more than 20 countries worldwide, which has enabled him to develop a unique playing style and coaching method.

His coaching philosophy revolves around three fundamental concepts: "best possible player conditioning," "quickness," and "conviction." These key points should be followed in every aspect of the game, but when they are followed in every aspect of life, a basketball player can become truly great.

There are thousands of drills that can be practiced to improve your basketball game. Even NBA players cannot pinpoint the exact programs that should be selected or discarded. However, with experience, seasoned coaches can give a guideline of drills most useful at the start of a new season. Thus, this book can be looked at as a summation of the most important lessons the author has meticulously taught his students for over 30 years.

Made in the USA
Monee, IL
08 March 2023

29425667R00031